4/15 44 (9/11)

CHOPIN

For Auntie Bertha
in loving memory of Valerie

First edition for the United States, Canada,
and the Philippines published 1993
by Barron's Educational Series, Inc.

Design David West Children's Book Design

Designed and produced by
Aladdin Books Ltd
28 Percy Street
London W1P 9FF

All inquiries should be addressed to:
Barron's Educational Series, Inc.
250 Wireless Boulevard
Hauppauge, NY 11788

International Standard Book No. 0-8120-1543-6

Library of Congress Catalog Card No. 92-30485

Library of Congress Cataloging-in-Publication Data
Rachlin, Ann.
    Chopin / by Ann Rachlin : illustrated by Susan Hellard.
        p. cm – (Famous children)
    Summary: Examines the childhood and early musical training of the
nineteenth-century Polish composer.
    ISBN 0-8120-1543-6
    1. Chopin, Frederic, 1810-1849–Childhood and youth–Juvenile
literature. 2. Composers–Biography–Juvenile literature.
[1. Chopin, Frederic, 1810-1849–Childhood and youth.
2. Composers.] I. Hellard, Susan, ill. II. Title. III. Series:
Rachlin, Ann. Famous children.
ML3930.C46R3 1993
786'.2–dc20   92-30485
[B]   CIP
                                                AC MN

Printed in Belgium
3456 987654321

Famous Children

CHOPIN

ANN RACHLIN
ILLUSTRATED BY SUSAN HELLARD

BARRON'S

"Stand up, Frederick! Shake hands with Mr. Zywny! He is your new piano teacher." Nicholas Chopin's voice was kind but firm and his little six-year-old son jumped to his feet. He loved playing the piano. His mother had been giving him music lessons since he was three. But now here was his new teacher. What would he be like?

Frederick held out his hand and looked at Albert Zywny. What a strange-looking man! He had a huge purple nose and, as he smiled at the little boy, Frederick saw that some of his teeth were missing. On his head was an untidy blond wig, which had slipped to one side. He wore yellow trousers and a yellow coat. But they were different yellows!

Frederick tried hard not to laugh when he saw Mr. Zywny's big boots. This curious man used his boots as a purse and there was money sticking out of the top. Mr. Zywny took off his frayed old cloak and sat down at the side of the piano.

"All right, Frederick," he said. "Let me hear you play!"

Frederick soon forgot how odd his teacher looked, for his music lessons were fascinating. He even got used to the strange smells. Mr. Zywny took snuff and scattered the strong powder everywhere – in his boots, on his cravat and especially on his vest. Mr. Zywny didn't believe in bathing either. On hot days he rubbed himself down with vodka!

Frederick adored Mr. Zywny. The boy was six years old and his teacher sixty, but they were soon firm friends. It seemed to the Chopins that Frederick's music lessons never ended for Mr. Zywny was so pleased with the little boy's progress that he stayed for hours, eating most of his meals with the family. As soon as each meal was over, Frederick raced back to the grand piano.

Frederick had three sisters, Louise, Isabella and Emilia. Their father was French. He had traveled to

Poland as a young man and was now housemaster of a boarding school in the Casimir Palace. His wife, Justina, was the housekeeper and looked after the pupils.

It was vacation time and Frederick was curled up in a chair with a piece of chocolate and a book.

"Father said we are going to the woods today!" announced Louise. Frederick loved going to the woods. It only took 15 minutes by carriage. Soon they were there, picking strawberries and hunting for mushrooms!

One evening, Frederick was reading aloud to the family when Mr. Zywny strode into the house.

"Guess what I've got here!" he said. With a flourish, he pulled out a printed sheet of music. Mr. Chopin leapt up and took a look.

"Why Frederick!" he exclaimed. "It's your Polish Dance! It says, 'Polonaise in G minor by Frederick Chopin'!" His father was beaming with pride.

Soon everyone in Warsaw was talking about the little Chopin boy. Only seven years old and composing! There was even an article in the *Warsaw Review* about him. It said, "The composer of this Polish Dance is the son of Nicholas Chopin, who teaches French and literature at the Lyceum School. The boy, who is only seven, is a real musical genius. Not only does he play the most difficult piano pieces but he also composes dances in a most outstanding way."

Now every day brought invitations. Mr. Zywny boasted to everyone about his clever pupil and made sure that all the important families in Warsaw read the

newspaper article. Soon every princess and countess wanted little Frederick to play at their parties. Mr. Chopin and Mr. Zywny accompanied Frederick, who was not shy at all. He enjoyed playing for the elegant ladies.

Just before his eighth birthday, Frederick gave his first concert in public. It was February 24, 1818. Wrapped in their beautiful cloaks, the most important people in Warsaw arrived by sleigh at the Radziwill Palace. Everyone clapped their hands as Frederick, dressed in a black velvet jacket with a huge white lace collar and short trousers with white stockings, walked onto the stage.

Frederick's fingers flew over the keys. The concerto by the Polish composer Gyrowetz was very difficult and the audience listened spellbound. At the end they jumped to their feet and applauded. Frederick slid off the piano stool and bowed. When he arrived home his mother asked,

"How did you get on, Frederick? What did they like best?"

"The white collar you made for me!" came the unexpected reply.

At that time, the Grand Duke Constantine ruled over Poland. He came from Russia and was a very cruel and bad-tempered man. Everyone was frightened of him. Sometimes he would leap into his carriage and race through the streets of Warsaw, firing his pistol in the air. The Grand Duke heard about Frederick and often sent his carriage to bring the little boy to the Belvedere Palace to play for him. Sometimes the Grand Duke was in a terrible rage when Frederick arrived, but as soon as the boy began to play the piano the Duke would calm down, soothed by the music.

Frederick often composed while he was playing for the Grand Duke. One day he began to create a new piece, his eyes raised to the ceiling.

"What are you looking up there for?" barked the irritable Duke. "Are the notes written on the ceiling?" Frederick took no notice and continued composing.

The piece that Frederick was composing was a military march. The Grand Duke began to relax. Soon he was smiling. Then there he was, marching up and down the drawing room, beating time to the music.

"Left! Right! Left! Right! I like this march!" he sang. He gave orders for it to be arranged for a huge military band. Frederick was very proud when he saw the soldiers marching to his music.

Frederick was very thin and the doctor decided that he should have a vacation in the country. Dominic, one of his school friends, invited him to stay in a lovely country village northwest of Warsaw.

Instead of sending letters home, Frederick wrote a newspaper describing all his vacation adventures. The newspaper was called the *Village Courier*.

A page from the *Village Courier:*

"We heard some important news today. The turkey laid its eggs behind the pantry."

"Yesterday the cat crept into a cupboard and broke a bottle of fruit juice. Luckily it was the smallest bottle!"

"Today one of the hens has gone lame and a drake had a fight with a goose."

Frederick Chopin could draw almost as well as he could play the piano. One day during a lesson at school, Frederick passed around his drawing of the teacher. It was a cartoon that made the master look very ugly. "Give me that piece of paper! Who drew this?" The teacher was angry. Frederick confessed and expected to be punished. But later that evening the drawing was returned with the words "Well drawn!" on the back.

Frederick Chopin became a great pianist and composed some of the most important music for the piano including 27 études, 25 preludes, 19 nocturnes, 52 mazurkas, 4 impromptus, and two piano concertos. Some of his pieces had nicknames:

The Minute Waltz was supposed to describe a dog chasing its tail.

The Raindrop Prelude sounds like the pitter-patter of the rain on the roof.

The Cat Waltz recalls the day when Chopin's cat jumped onto the keyboard and ran up and down the keys.